Teach Your Child to Be Successful at Anything
Even Math

ISBN: 9798887579771

For Arrows Learning
www.forarrowslearning.com

Printed in the United States of America

Table of Contents

Chapter 1

Introduction

Chapter 2

The Biggest Misconception About Learning Math

Chapter 3

5 Steps to Math Success

Chapter 4

Maintaining and Expanding Success

Chapter 5

Hurdles on the Road to Success

Chapter 6

Conclusion

Bonus

Homework Help Cheat Sheet

Introduction

As a mother of four and an educator for over a decade, I have encountered some fairly intense cases of math hatred. One year, on the first day of school, as I was explaining the beauty and value of math, a student volunteered to show the class just how beautiful he thought math was. He asked if he could go up to the board to explain his point to the class. I enthusiastically handed him a dry erase marker, excited about what he was going to write. This is what he wrote: "MATH = **M**ental **A**buse **T**o **H**umans." I gasped with shock, and then we all laughed. I turned to the class and told them I would soon change their minds about math, and for most, if not all of them, I did.

My oldest son did not think of math as a form of mental abuse, but he did believe he wasn't good at it. He felt that he just wasn't "gifted" in math. This doubly broke my heart, both as a mother and also as a math teacher of course. I never want my children or my students to put limits on their abilities. Yet my son believed that no matter how hard he tried, he just would not be able to do well in math. Does this sound familiar? Thankfully, he no longer feels this way and he now even enjoys math. I want that same success for your child too.

How would you like to change your child's mind about learning math? Wouldn't it be wonderful for them to say, "Math class wasn't so bad today," or "I learned something interesting in math today..."? Well, that's my goal. I want to share my tips and tricks on how you can help your child learn to succeed in math.

Notice that I said, "learn to succeed." I put it this way because success does not just happen. It must be taught. Here's the thing: math does not have to be their favorite subject. Nevertheless, using the information shared in this book will at least help them realize that math is doable.

Math is typically the most hated of all the subjects students encounter in school. If you are able to help your child in math, other subjects could easily follow suit. The insights you gain here can be readily adapted to any subject, although for present purposes we will focus on math.

I am excited for us to go on this journey together as we explore how to teach your child to be successful at anything, even math.

Sincerely,

Yvonne Chimwaza

"...success does not just happen. It must be taught."

The Biggest Misconception About Learning Math

You might think that if your child does not excel at math now, that will always be the case. The truth is it does not have to be. This aversion to math is most likely math anxiety.[1] The first step in children overcoming their math anxiety is you, as a parent, believing or at least hoping that they can.

I am reminded of a young lady who always tried hard, but still struggled with math. Somehow her high school course schedule was mistakenly rearranged, and she was erroneously placed in Honors Geometry. It was the only geometry class available, so there wasn't the option of moving to a class at a lower level. She was terrified but determined. This young lady, her mother, and her teacher all believed that her determination would help her pass the class. Sure enough, at the end of course both the student and her teacher cried for joy, because she did in fact pass.

[1] In some instances, difficulty in math may be caused by an underlying learning disability. The information shared here should still be applicable, but should be used in addition to the guidance given by your child's medical professional.

This same young lady ended up excelling in her college math classes by applying that same determination. She went from struggling to excelling, all because others believed in her and she believed in herself. It is possible to excel at math, even if it is not your strength.

The number one reason that students do not succeed at math is because they lose motivation and give up. It is vital that you help your child's mindset change in order that they might be successful. We will talk a little more about this later.

"The number one reason that students do not succeed at math is because they lose motivation and give up."

5 Steps to Math Success
Adjust Your Speech About Math

Hello, Parent/Aunt/Uncle/Guardian! This first step is for you. It's pop quiz time! Please answer the following questions truthfully. 1) Have you ever made a comment such as, "I was never good at math"? 2) Have you ever complained in the hearing of your child that you do not know how to do math the way it is taught today? 3) Have you ever said something like, "After middle school, math is useless. All you need to know is how to add, subtract, and a few other things..."? If you answered yes to any of these questions or had to hesitate a little before saying no, this next piece of advice is definitely for you!

What I have to say might be difficult to hear, but it's easy to change, so be prepared. Dear Parent/Aunt/Uncle/Guardian, you have added to your child's math anxiety. Ouch, right? These words are a bit uncomfortable, but they are true. The words we say carry a tremendous amount of weight in the lives of our children. I can prove it to you. Think about your child's conversations with others. How often do you hear them repeating things about themselves that you have said? Whether it be baby stories or character evaluations, I am sure that you have heard your own words come out of their mouths. I once said to my husband that our second born was witty and quick with his responses. I later overheard my son (then five years old) telling his grandmother that he was witty.

He repeated what he heard me say about him and my words became a part of his identity. Our words are caretakers, forming the way our children view their abilities, whether it be perceived strengths or weaknesses. If your child hears you say that math is unimportant or impossible this will become their philosophy too.

"Our words are caretakers, forming the way our children view their abilities..."

Thankfully, all we have to do is start speaking differently to and about our children, especially about math. It might seem like a very small thing, but it can have a huge impact. Perhaps you are thinking, "So how do I fix this?" Well, here are a few practical tips on improving this.

- *Share the honest truth about your math struggles, but also how you overcame them to be where you are now.* This could be something like, "I was never very good at math, but I worked hard at it (or wish that I had worked hard at it). I'm sure that with hard work you will be great at it."
- *Make comments, not judgements.* Instead of saying, "The way they teach math today doesn't make sense," say, "Wow, I never learned it that way, you must have the updated version." This still communicates that the teaching is different, but not that it is wrong or bad. If your child thinks the math they are learning is wrong or bad, they will not be motivated to excel. Additionally, they will convey your thoughts to their teacher and to others who may otherwise try to help them understand math better.
- *Confirm that math is an important subject.* The Greek origin of the word mathematics is mathema which means "to learn." Math helps us take "difficult" concepts or situations and find solutions for them. In other words, math trains us to

develop problem-solving skills. I am sure we can all agree that difficult situations and circumstances go beyond our school experiences and follow us as we continue with adult life. Why not give your child a leg up in the world by encouraging them to learn problem-solving skills through math? Math develops these problem-solving skills and builds grit, which we will talk about a bit more in the next section.

Get Grit

Grit is something that all successful people have and something that every math student needs. I like to define grit as the determination to accomplish something despite the challenges it brings. Grit does not develop if we never encounter obstacles; it is formed instead through overcoming those obstacles. Math teaches grit and to develop this grit means there will be some challenges that should not be shied away from.

It is hard to watch our little ones struggle in any area of their lives. We are built with a desire to protect them, so it is only natural for us to try and remove or minimize the obstacle or challenge that they are facing. However, the reality is that we must let them problem solve for themselves. As a teacher, I always know when the parent, older sibling, or calculator "helped" a little too much on homework or a project. This is because the student would not be able to produce the same results if faced with the same task in my classroom. Do I still give the student the participation grade for homework or the "A" on the project? Of course. But as that old southern saying goes, "What the wash don't catch the rinse will." In other words, they may have gained a top score for the project, but a test or quiz score will reveal that they do not yet fully understand the concept.

To fully grasp concepts in math, your child will need to become more comfortable, not just with making mistakes as they learn, but with correcting mistakes. That is grit. Many students who struggle with math become comfortable about making mistakes, but they feel that they are helpless to correct them. I remember tutoring a young man in college algebra.

"Grit is something that all successful people have and something that every math student needs."

Much of the math material was a review from high school Algebra II and Advanced Math. Prior to our session, he told me that he was bad at math and that he made a lot of mistakes. I remember saying, "Mistakes are good as long as you learn from them and correct them." As we moved through the concepts and as I explained them, his eyes grew wide and he would look at me and say, "Bruh!" in complete disbelieve that he now understood the concept. I chuckled every time it happened because I could see the lightbulbs turning on in his head as his confidence grew with every conquered math problem. By the end of our session, if he made a mistake, he would retrace his steps and begin to correct it with little to no help from me. That is the power of grit and it extends far beyond the confines of a math question. When your child develops grit, they will become more resilient, a trait that will take them far in life.

So, perhaps you are wondering, "How do I help my child build grit? I've changed the way I talk about math and now I am ready to see them persevere." Building grit is all about small wins and below are a few useful tips for creating those for your child.

- *Give them a task or goal that is slightly difficult, but attainable, regardless of whether it is math related or not.* Then let them feel the experience of successfully conquering the challenge. The most important thing about the task you choose is that they can accomplish it. Maybe you can ask them to help you with the monthly budget, or estimate what the grocery total will be, or tally the tip at a restaurant. The goal can be directed to something that caters to their interests. If they are interested in building and have the skills to build a birdhouse, then you can ask them to build one. If they are into video games, perhaps encourage them to try beating that next level (after their math homework, of course). Be sure to explain that since they dug deep and conquered one difficult thing, they can apply that same grit to conquering math also. Whatever you decide to do, make sure that they win on their own at something "hard."

- *Give them a good old-fashioned motivational speech*. I remember almost every single one of my teachers giving some version of the "Michael Jordan" talk. It went something like this: "Do you think that Michael Jordan was instantly great at basketball? No, he worked for it. On days he was tired, he worked. On days he felt defeated, he worked. He never gave up. Say 'never give up.' Say it again loudly, 'NEVER GIVE UP!'" That story got me every single time. Even though basketball was not my thing, I was convinced that hard work, grit if you will, could and would help me accomplish anything. Remember, your words to your child are powerful.

- *Do not run to their rescue at the first sign of difficulty.* As we discussed earlier, it is hard to watch our children struggle, but we know it is necessary. We are not helping them by giving them the answers. If you find them struggling quite a bit with a topic, ask questions that will help them arrive at the proper answer. Those questions should sound like, "What is the question asking for? What information is already given? Does this look like something else you have solved? If so, how did you solve it the previous time?" These types of questions will help them discover the answer on their own and build grit.

Actively Make Math Fun

When I taught math, my students thought that I lived, ate, and breathed math 24/7. No matter the grade level, I always heard my students say, "Man, she really loves math." The truth of the matter is —and please do not tell my former students—I did not love math as much as it seemed. However, I knew that math needed to be fun and engaging if they were to learn it. As the beloved and famous fictional character, Mary Poppins, once said, "A spoon full of sugar helps the medicine go down." We can apply this philosophy to many areas of life and math education should be no different.

People like to do the things that they like to do. I know it sounds simple, but it is true for your child too. Find a way to make math something that they like to do. There are so many free and paid mathematical games available online to help students see math as a reward instead of a duty. There are engaging videos, courses and other resources that can help students engage with math. If you can find what they are interested in, there is most likely a way to connect it to math. Making math fun and engaging is not as difficult as it seems, you just need to look in the right places. Next are a few suggestions on where to start.

"People like to do the things that they like to do... Find a way to make math something that they like to do."

- *Ask your child's teacher to recommend engaging supplemental material.* If you homeschool, you can ask others in your co-op, or follow a homeschool group on social media to ask questions and get ideas. Teachers will most likely have a host of resources that they use at school or would recommend and will gladly tell you all about them. Your child's success also has an effect on teachers' yearly evaluations, so they have a vested interest in addition to simply wanting children to succeed.
- *Do an online search for math games, fun math support, or fun math videos.* Again, it is a simple task, but one that can yield great results and resources and many of them are free.
- *Check your local library or museum for STEAM (Science Technology Engineering Art and Math) events.* There are free math-related events happening all the time, even in small cities or towns. Events like these can allow your child to be around other young students who enjoy math, and that experience can inspire your child.

Vigorously Learn with Them and From Them

Everyone loves the feeling of imparting information to someone who is genuinely interested in what they have to say. Think how it makes you feel when you are showing the "new guy" at work how to do something and he says, "Wow, that is amazing." How does it make you feel? I am sure it makes you feel you have something of value to give others through your skill. The same is true of children. My children light up when they feel they can teach me something or when I ask for their advice or opinion on a topic. It gives them a sense of pride and value.

Think about the impact you can have on your child if you let them teach you the math they are learning, or learn along with them. Allowing your child to feel like the expert could eventually help them become one, even if it is not in math. (Side note: This will also open an opportunity for your child and you to connect on a different level and could deepen your relationship.) Take it from an educator, it feels great when you get to teach someone who wants to learn from you and who understands what you are teaching. Creating opportunities for your child to teach you is very easy and we will look at a few ways of doing this next.

"Allowing your child to feel like the expert could eventually help them become one..."

- *Carve out time to sit and learn with them.* Clear your calendar and remove as many distractions as possible to spend 15 - 30 minutes learning with and from your child. If time and attention span allow for more than 30 minutes, then by all means go for it. This can be a daily, twice weekly, or weekly event, but the more time you invest this small amount of time, the better.

- *Ask them what they learned in math today.* If you need a starting point, ask them what they learned that day or what they have been reviewing. Ask them to explain it to you if they understand it. If you are familiar with the concept, let them teach you their way of doing it. If they cannot remember, look at their class notebook. You can also email their teacher ahead of time, so you will have the information when it's needed.

- *Learn concepts together that they do not understand.* Even if you know how to solve the question, look it up with them. Review their notes from class, find an online video, or search their textbook to see how the problem is solved. Then patiently ask your child to explain it. You have to be very sensitive and encouraging here because you do not want them to feel defeated while trying to explain it. Be sure to incorporate some of the grit-building techniques to help with this.

Eagerly Celebrate Every Small Success

Remember when we were discussing grit and how it is vital for your child to experience small wins? Well, the final component is to celebrate those wins. A little celebration goes a long way. Tell them how amazing they are doing. Tell them how much grit they have developed. Tell them what an amazing teacher they are. Celebrating them will have a similar effect as letting them teach you. It will help them feel valuable and successful. Even if others do not measure what they have accomplished as a success, you have, and that means the world to them. If they made a 35 on their last math quiz and this time made a 50, celebrate the progress and reach out to the teacher for feedback and suggestions on how to make even more progress. If you are your child's teacher, then give them honest, but positive feedback.

Celebrating the successes does not mean ignoring how far they are from where they need to be. But it does mean that your affirmation is not limited to them passing or not. Celebrate them while at the same time building grit. This sounds like, "Yes! We have met this goal! I am so proud of you, and I knew you could do it. You will just keep going up from here as long as you keep working hard." Remember back in step one, when we discussed the weight that your negative words about math can carry? Well, your positive words can carry just as much, if not more. Think back to those one or those two teachers who believed in you and poured into your life so much that you still remember their names and how they made you feel. You have that same opportunity to champion your child on their math journey. You may be thinking to yourself, "I am not a cheerleader, I'm a realist and the world will not cheer for them." Well if the world will not, then it is imperative that you do! Yes, teach them the realities of life, but also be their biggest cheerleader. Up next are some tips on how to do so.

"A little celebration goes
a long way."

- Fight to see the glass as half full even when it is a quarter full. In other words, look for the smallest ounce of accomplishment to celebrate. If they complete their homework when they have been inconsistent with doing so in the past, then celebrate the fact that they completed it this time. Purposefully look for anything and everything to celebrate.
- Verbal praise works wonders. Verbal praise is one of the easiest ways to celebrate your child, but it must be specific and sincere. It should sound something like, "Great job on _____, and the way that you did _____ to accomplish _____. It was amazing and I am so proud of you." If praise is not specific and sincere it will not have the desired effect.
- Rewards are another great way to celebrate successes. Rewards do not have to be new gaming systems. They can be as simple as, "Wow, you passed your math test today, great job! How about you pick what we are having for dinner tonight," or "Let's stop by the store and get that comic book you have been wanting." I do not suggest using rewards every time, because they need to feel like a special treat and not an entitlement. However, rewards do help to validate success.

How To Sustain Our Success: AGAVE

Now that you know how to help your child become successful at math, your next question is probably *how do I sustain the success? How do I maintain their confidence and willingness to try in math?* I wish there was a special tea or secret sauce I could give you, but I do have one sweet tip for maintaining your child's success, and it is all about "AGAVE."

Agave is a delicious and sweet substitute for sugar that is believed to be a healthier option. Before you think I have gone completely off topic by bringing up a sugar substitute, let me explain. Previously I mentioned Mary Poppins' philosophy about sweetening the taste of medicine. Well here is a philosophy for sweetening math: Add AGAVE to make math great every day. So, what is AGAVE? It stands for **A**djust Your Speech About Math, **G**et Grit, **A**ctively Make Math Fun, **V**igorously Learn with Them and From Them, and **E**agerly Celebrate Every Small Success. AGAVE is an acronym that will help you remember the steps to success and keep you consistent.

Consistency is the key to all successful ventures and your child's success is no different. Find a way to keep

AGAVE always at the forefront of your mind. Revisit it. Practice it. Be consistent. Your willingness to constantly practice the skills you have gained will ensure that they stick and that your child will continue to succeed. One way to do this is by creating a poster or vision board with your child about AGAVE that you hang in your home. You may even decide to create an AGAVE morning affirmation that you say together every day.

"Add AGAVE to make math great every day."

Applying AGAVE to Other Subjects

AGAVE can be adapted for every area of your child's education and life. With a few small adjustments, AGAVE can be applied to English, Science, History, Physical Education or anything else. If your child is trying to achieve the Presidential Fitness Award this school year, for example, then **Adjust** your speech about fitness. **Get** Grit by helping them accomplish small fitness wins (two pull ups instead of just one). **Actively** make fitness fun by looking up funny online fitness videos. **Vigorously** learn with and from them by practicing the exercises they are doing at school to the best of your ability and letting them explain them. **Eagerly** celebrate every small success by cheering them on every time they shave a second off their mile time. It's that easy! The principles of AGAVE can be adapted to other subjects and can become a way of life.

Live In the Present

The fastest way to stop your child's progress is to live in the past. Spending too much time and energy focusing on the past can be damaging. Comments such as, "You don't want to end up failing like you were before," or "You don't want to start being bad at math again," could make them believe that they have not changed, and that failure is inevitable. The only reason to revisit the past is to focus on success. It is fine and important to speak about how much growth they have experienced, but do not suggest that they can go back to being the person they used to be. Do not let a moment of frustration, disappointment, or anything cause you to undo the success you have worked so hard to achieve by using the past as a weapon. Use AGAVE instead.

Hurdles on the Road to Success

We all know that hurdles and obstacles are a part of life. So, how do you handle seeing your child's journey to success in math slow down because of hurdles and obstacles? The answer is to double down on AGAVE. Do a quick assessment of why there is a slowdown. It is possible it has absolutely nothing to do with math and that there is something else going on. Ask your child how they feel about their success in math. Find out how their relationships with their friends are going and how their other classes are progressing. If you find that math is not the only hurdle they are facing, then handle the others accordingly. If the problem is solely with math, then reach out to your child's teacher to find additional fun resources, or get their advice on how to help with the topic that is being covered.

The other hurdle that you may encounter is a failed assessment. The advice here is the same, double down on AGAVE, especially the "E": **Eagerly** Celebrate Every Small Success. You do this by celebrating the simple fact that they were confident enough to at least try the test. Think about it, they could have just written "IDK" and turned in their assignment. Instead, they tried and that should be celebrated. Our goal is to get them to believe that they can and be willing to try without anxiety. If they are doing those things the grades will follow.

"Our goal is to get them
to believe that they can
and be willing to try
without anxiety."

Conclusion

Math does not have to be seen as "Mental Abuse To Humans" as my student once wrote on my board. Your child can be successful at math as long as they believe in themselves and are willing to try. With your help and by applying the principles of AGAVE, you will set your child up for success, and thereafter the sky is the limit to what they will accomplish. One young man once shared with me that finally understanding math is what opened the doors for him to complete college and go into the medical field. Math can and will open many doors in your child's future, so help them learn to be successful at math. Just remember to add AGAVE to make math great every day. You've got this!

Homework Help
Cheat Sheet

Homework Help Cheat Sheet

5 Quick Tips for increased patience when helping your child with homework.

Stay Positive

No matter how stressed or tired you feel maintain positivity.

Body Language

Your body language must match your words. Sit up. Make eye contact. Lean in.

Deep Breath

If you feel stressed take a deep, but subtle breath to have time to form a positive, calm response.

Ask Questions

Don't give them answers. If they get stuck ask them questions that will lead them to the right answer.

Send A Message

If additional support is needed send an email or letter to your child's teacher, about needing homework support.

Yvonne Chimwaza Serves as the owner and Parent Engagement Specialist at For Arrows Learning. For Arrows Learning provides training and resources to promote student and parental involvement in the student's education. Through children's books, parent/educator courses, eBooks, and parental engagement consulting it inspires students and empower parents to increase students' confidence in mathematics and beyond.

Yvonne has been an educator for over a decade, beginning as a middle school math teacher and continuing to teach math courses for grades 6th-12th. As a teacher, Yvonne was selected as Teacher of the Year for two consecutive years at two different schools on the basis of her aptitude for engaging parents and inspiring students. Moreover, Yvonne has had experience as a homeschool teacher and learning coach.
She has had multiple opportunities to provide professional development to educators.

She has written multiple articles including, "Math is Not Your Enemy: 4 Tips to Combat Student Math Anxiety" featured in STEM Magazine's February 2020 issue. In addition, she has written a children's book: The Big Math Lie and an accompanying online course for this book, Teach Your Child To Be Successful at Anything, Even Math. Yvonne consulted with Staples in 2020 to provide virtual teaching tips for teachers forced to teach remotely due to the COVID-19 pandemic.

Yvonne holds a Masters of Natural Science degree with a concentration in math education from Louisiana State University. She enjoys writing, watching documentaries, and spending time with her family, especially her husband and four children.

We can't wait to hear about your child's success!

Visit our website to share your success stories and learn about upcoming products.

www.forarrowslearning.com

www.ingramcontent.com/pod-product-compliance
Lightning Source LLC
Chambersburg PA
CBHW051559120626
46551CB00013B/1585